SPOOKY CREEPY CUTIES

A COLORING ADVENTURE FOR TEENS AND ADULTS

DREAMWHIRL

DREAMWHIRL

Dear Coloring Enthusiast,

Welcome to the delightfully eerie realm of Creepy Cuties Coloring Book, where every stroke of your pen reveals the playful yet spooky inhabitants of our enchanting world. As you embark on this peculiar journey, prepare to immerse yourself in a realm where adorable meets eerie, beckoning forth your inner artist to awaken and embrace the unconventional.

Within the pages of this bewitching Humorous, you'll discover a curated collection of 50 spine-tingling illustrations, each eagerly awaiting your creative touch. From mischievous creatures to haunted abodes and curious culinary delights, every page is a canvas brimming with potential, beckoning you to explore the shadows and breathe life into our charmingly peculiar inhabitants.

Embrace the unexpected with our unique reverse coloring approach, a twisted take on tradition that empowers you to color beyond the lines and unleash your imagination in ways both thrilling and unconventional. Dive into the darkness and let your creativity run wild, as you bring forth vibrant hues to illuminate the eerie beauty of each design.

Whether you seek a moment of macabre mindfulness or a surge of artistic inspiration, the Creepy Cuties Coloring Book promises to be your eerie sanctuary. Lose yourself in the whimsical world of our creepy cuties, finding solace and joy in the act of coloring as you explore the shadows and embrace the strange.

We trust that this coloring book will become a cherished companion on your journey of self-discovery and artistic exploration. May it bring you moments of delightful chills, inspiration, and pure, eerie delight as you breathe life into each page.

Happy coloring!

DreamWhirl

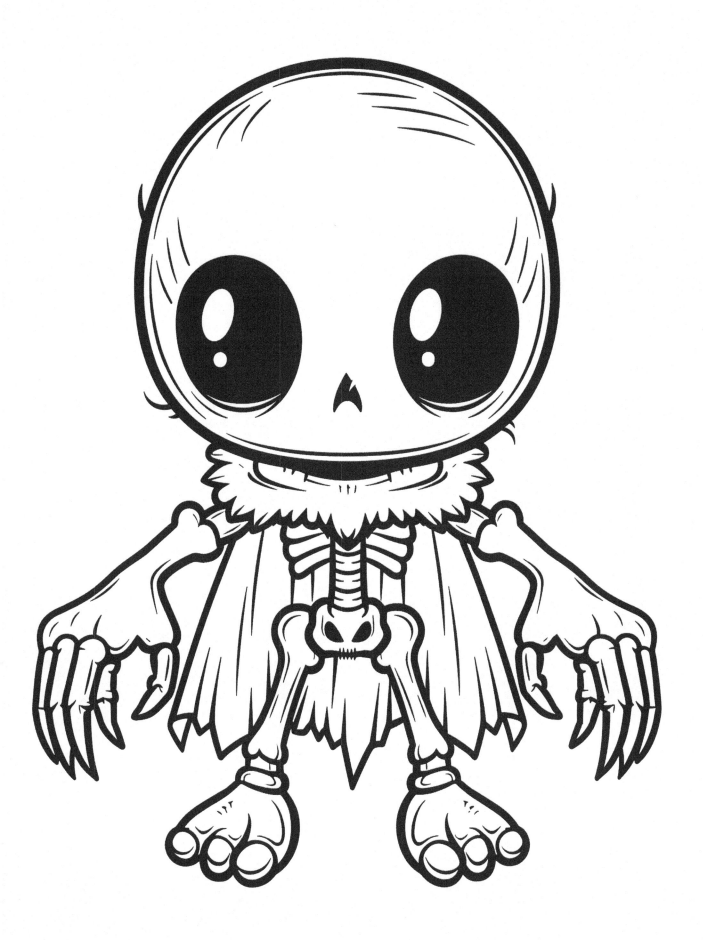

Made in the USA
Las Vegas, NV
29 December 2024

15558854R10059